A Quarter'S Worth of

HumoR

James Brigleb

All the world's a stage,
And all the men and women merely players:
They have their exits and their entrances;
And one man in his time plays many parts…
William Shakespeare

Laugh, and the world laughs with you; weep, and you weep alone
Ella Wheeler Wilcox

For those of us who are teachers, our world is a bit of a stage. Our students arrive, and like it or not, they expect a performance. We're on from the time they filter into the room until the last one leaves at the end of the day. It can be exhausting for both parties.

Further, Wilcox's line is so true in the classroom, perhaps moreso with adolescents and teenagers than with elementary age students. Nobody enjoys a whining teacher (unless you consider the whiner himself – he probably likes the whining). Unfortunately, it's not always true that if the teacher laughs, the whole class laughs along. In fact, far too often, students stare in disbelief, disdain, or embarrassment of my attempts to get them to enjoy "the ride." Oh well, just adds to the fun of being developmentally arrested.

But in all seriousness, being serious all the time just isn't that much fun. So, whether you're an educator or a normal person, I hope you enjoy the jokes, anecdotes, and stories shared in this book, and in turn, tell them to others.

People like to smile, they like to laugh, and our world needs a bit of levity. Why not be a person who can help bring that about with good, clean fun?

A disclaimer: NONE of the jokes, stories, anecdotes, or lists are my *original* material. They have either been told to me, sent to me, or found by me in a variety of places. But in all cases (like most jokes) the originator never got the credit that he or she deserves – they have all been heard, told, or read as anonymous. In many cases, I have altered the content to fit my own style and audience.

How to Tell a Joke

At the risk of insulting you, the reader, I feel the need to address the subject of *delivery*. I have witnessed absolutely hilarious jokes or stories fall flat on their inorganic faces due to a failure on the part of the "teller" to bring life to the content.

At least half the enjoyment the audience derives from a joke is not the actual lines of the story. No, it's the antics and theatrics of the person delivering the joke, story, or anecdote.

Accordingly, those of you who plan on sharing these with an audience – whether that audience be students, colleagues, coworkers, or general public – the need to understand that the material is only half (at best) the equation. Listeners enjoy voice, timing, facial expressions, gestures, and relationship. This is not to imply that you have to be a professional comedian to tell a good joke. But you do need to let go of some of those natural inhibitions that plague us – telling us to play it safe and nobody gets hurt. Instead, as a "teller," we need to put ourselves into the story. It needs to be told as if we were truly involved in the situation at hand.

If you want to make the most of sharing these, spend a bit of time thinking about the timing, practice voices, allow natural facial expressions to surface. I've found the biggest inhibitor of telling a great story is studying the faces of my audience, seeking approval, while I'm in the midst of the telling. The tendency is then to reflect the mood and attitude of the audience.

What we need to do is divorce ourselves from the listeners. For those of you who have been on stage before, this is familiar. Actors, on stage, are taught about a "wall" that separates themselves from the audience. It is as if they are acting within a vacuum. Intellectually, the actor knows the audience is there, but s/he must put out 100% irrespective of the response from those watching the performance. And so it is for the storyteller.

So, Mr. or Ms. Storyteller, cut loose. Figure out how you'd like to tell the story – how you'd like to hear it, should somebody be telling it to you. Rehearse it. Then, present it to your audience. Don't look for their approval as you're performing. But know this: most of the time your audience will want to hear more.

Dedication

This is dedicated to my family – particularly my wife, Linda. How many corny jokes have you listened to me tell? Thanks for humoring me and telling me I'm funny. I love to make each of you laugh!

So, thank you Linda, Elisabeth, Alison, Rebekah, and Jack!
You guys are the best!

Contents

Contents, continued

Day 1

*This is a great joke to tell on the first day meeting a group –
especially if you're like me and have trouble remembering names. Like
all the jokes, this is enhanced through theatrics – assume the facial
expressions of the characters, use body language to "act out" the parts.*

The Bell Ringer

Once upon a time there was a guy named Quasimodo. His job
was chief bell ringer. Well, he died, leaving Notre Dame without
someone to ring the bell in the belfry, announcing the times of the day.

Notre Dame ran an ad in the "Help Wanted" section of the
Middle Ages Times, advertising for a new bell ringer.

A week later, an applicant showed up to apply, but this guy
didn't have any arms.

The priest invited the man in, but, of course, wanted to know,
"How, in the world, would you be able to ring the bell? It weighs a
bloody ton. The bell ringer must use all of his strength while grabbing
the rope, pulling mightily, and repeating the deed as many as twelve
times at one stint."

The applicant seemed unfazed. "May I demonstrate?"

So, the priest and the applicant climbed many flights of stairs,
and arrived up in the belfry – which was a good 100 feet or more above
the ground.

The applicant backed away from the bell (as far as the small space would allow), proceeded to run at bell, jumped, and collided with the bell using his face. The bell made a most impressive gong.

The priest was, indeed, impressed. "But how do I know you can keep this up? I mean, that was most appealing (get it?). But what about later on? What you just did would suffice for one o'clock. But what happens when it's, say, three or four o'clock? I'm going to need proof that you have the stamina for the job."

So, the applicant backed away from the bell, ran at it and repeated the process. The bell made a most satisfying gong. Backing away, he proceeded to repeat his actions.

At this point, the priest was feeling a little bit guilty, and a little queasy. He wasn't sure if he could watch the applicant do this twelve times, even if capable. "One more time, please," said the priest. "So I can be sure."

The applicant backed away, ran at the bell, and…missed. He proceeded to fall from the belfry tower, all 100 feet or so, and impacted the cobblestone, thus meeting his death.

Below, several stunned peasants surrounded the body. The priest looked down from above. Someone in the crowd asked, "Who was he?"

The priest looked down upon the group and shouted back, "I don't know, but his face sure rings a bell!"

Well, a week later, another applicant showed up for the job. Amazingly, like the first applicant, the second applicant had no arms.

Further, it turned out that the second applicant was the first applicant's brother.

The priest said "There is absolutely no way I can allow you to apply – especially given what already has happened to your brother."

The second applicant says, "Listen, you don't understand. In my family, the younger brother MUST carry on in his older brother's place. It is a matter of honor. If I were to return home being turned away from fulfilling my brother's calling, I would become the disgrace of my family, and my family the disgrace of our village. Please, give me a chance. I must be allowed to ring for my brother!"

So, against his better judgment, the priest allowed the request. He took the brother up into the belfry for a tryout. The brother, at seeing the bell, realized this was where his brother met his fate, became overcome with sadness, stumbled backward, and fell off the belfry.

Below, looking at the lifeless body, was the same group of peasants. They called up to the priest, "This man, too, has no arms! What was his name?"

The priest looked down and hollered, "I'm not sure. All I know is – surely, he's a dead ringer for his brother!"

Day 2

Jokes are not the only kind of humor an audience will enjoy. Whether spoken, illuminated as a revolving PowerPoint, or given as a handout to your audience, **Tom Swifties** *provide a double entendre, which stimulate and toy with the mind.*

Tom Swifties

"It's too hot in here," said Tom *heatedly*.

"I heard a body washed up on the shore of one of the Great Lakes," said Tom *eerily*.

"I'm doing research on the atmospheric conditions over the Great Lakes," said Tom with an air of *Superiority*.

"What a neat guillotine," said Tom *off the top of his head*.

"We're out of dish soap," said Tom *Joylessly*.

"I really need a haircut," said Tom *harriedly*.

"Lassie, come back with that cantaloupe!" said Tom with a tone of *melancholy*.

"Nurse, cancel my appointments today," said Dr. Tom *impatiently*.

"Would you like a 7-Up?" asked Tom *spritely*.

"I guess I've put on a few pounds," said Tom *expansively*.

"I need some fresh air!" Tom *vented*.

"I just spent two hours in a traffic jam!" said Tom *exhaustedly*.

"Well, I finally got this uniform on," said Tom, *fatigued*.

"I just ran over Garfield!" said Tom *categorically*.

"I'm sure it's poison oak," said Tom *rashly*.

"We must find the bones of the first man," said Tom *adamantly*.

Day 3

Poor cats – Seems like everybody enjoys picking on felines these days. But seriously, they deserve it. I mean, what is it about having a pet that 50% of the population is allergic to, enjoys shredding your furniture, covers its toilet with its paws, strolls on the kitchen counter, sleeps in the napkin basket after walking across the dining table, scratches one's children walking down the hall, regularly leaves the owner's premises to find another cat to fight so that you can take it to the vet to have abscesses drained, and then treats you like it is doing you a huge favor by allowing you to live in your home? We've had six.

How to Bathe a Cat

1. Thoroughly clean the toilet.

2. Lift both lids and add shampoo.

3. Find and soothe the cat as you carry it to the bathroom.

4. In one swift move, place cat in toilet, close both lids and sit on top, so cat cannot escape.

5. The cat will self-agitate and produce ample suds (ignore ruckus from inside the toilet, as the cat is enjoying this.)

6. Flush toilet 3 - 4 times. This provides a power rinse - quite effective.

7. Have someone open outside door, stand as far from toilet as possible, and quickly lift both lids.

8. Clean cat will rocket out of the toilet to the outdoors, where he will air dry.

Sincerely, The Dog

Day 4

I love the vernacular and nuances that grew from the Valley Girl era. It's so much fun to imitate and embellish. The story below gains at least half the humor from the characterization of the girls involved. So, ham it up – your audience will love it.

Gullible Teenage Daughter

One of my daughters got into a car accident this summer and thought what she had was a minor fender bender. So as to appear responsible, she immediately drove to the body shop. The owner sized her up pretty quickly as being young and impressionable. "Can I help you?" he asked, greeting her by the car.

"Yeah, I just, like, got into an accident and need to know what this is going to cost," she confided.

"Well, let's take a look," said the mechanic. After doing some calculations, he said, "It's going to be about $2000 to fix."

"Two thousand dollars!" exclaimed my daughter. "That's, like, a lot of money!"

"Yes, it is," agreed the mechanic, "but there's not too much I can do about it. That's just what it costs to fix this."

"Isn't there some cheaper way to, like, fix it?" she complained.

"Well," said the mechanic, "there is a do-it-yourself solution."

"There is?" my daughter became greatly interested.

"Yep, you could take it home, wait for the engine and exhaust system to cool off, put your mouth over the tailpipe and blow as hard as you can. Sometimes that re-inflates the car and straightens the dents right out."

My daughter was suspicious. "Like, what do you take me for? An idiot?"

"Hey, I'm just trying to help. Take the advice or leave it."

My daughter drove home, waited about 30 minutes and then went back out and looked at the car. She felt the tailpipe, and it was cool. She looked around to make sure no one was watching, then got down, put her mouth on the tailpipe and blew for all she was worth. Of course, nothing happened. She tried again - nothing.

About that time, her roommate pulled in the driveway. "Like, what happened to your car?!?" she said, somewhat alarmed.

"Duh! Can't you see? I, like, got into an accident."

"Oh-MY-Gosh. You are so, like, busted! But, what are you, like, doing?" the roommate asked.

"Hello?!? Everybody knows if you blow into the tailpipe, the pressure will, like, re-inflate the car and the dents will, like, go away."

The roommate shook her head. "What – are you, like, blonde or something? It's not going to work. So *hello* right back."

My daughter asked, "Hello, *why* not?'

Her roommate finished, "Hello. I'm so sure. Because the windows on your car are, like, DOWN. Duh!"

Day 5

This next entry provides some opportunity to introduce vocabulary that students are exposed to on an increasing basis, but may not really understand. When I introduce the clinical terms first, and give examples, or ask for examples (if students know), I can then proceed with the joke. Middle school kids feel greatly empowered by this information. Of course, this vocabulary step would be unnecessary with an adult audience, but the humor is enjoyed none-the-less.

While some might say the joke is not funny given the disorders, it's one of the situations where I find it helps to laugh. Otherwise, life gets too depressing.

Welcome to the Psychiatric Hotline

If you are obsessive compulsive - press 1 repeatedly.

If you are codependent - ask someone to press 2.

If you have multiple personalities - press 3, 4, 5, and 6.

If you are paranoid - we know who you are and are tracing this call.

If you are schizophrenic - a little voice will tell you what to do.

If you are depressed - it doesn't matter what you do, nobody cares anyway.

Day 6

*Do you remember the days of sitting around in college saying, "Have you ever thought about...?" or "I wonder what would happen if...?" Well, usually those conversations were meant to be kind of **heavy**. So occasionally, it's fun to ponder the ridiculous. Whether you choose to project, read, or lace your discussion with the following thought provokers, they usually bring smiles to faces. With students, it's fun to introduce these, as many of them have never experienced this kind of silliness.*

Heavy Questions

1. If a librarian tells you where the self-help books are, does that defeat the purpose?

2. What if there were no hypothetical questions?

3. If a deaf person swears, does his mother wash his hands with soap?

4. If someone with multiple personalities threatens to kill himself, is it considered a hostage situation?

5. Why is there an expiration date on sour cream?

6. What's another word for synonym?

7. Where do forest rangers go to "get away from it all"?

8. What do you do when you see an endangered animal eating an endangered plant?

9. If you ate both pasta and antipasto, would you still be hungry?

10. Would a fly without wings be called a *walk*?

11. If a turtle doesn't have a shell, is he homeless or naked?

12. Can vegetarians eat animal crackers?

13. If the police arrest a mime, do they tell him he has the right to remain silent?

14. Why do they put Braille on the drive-through bank machines?

15. How do they get deer to cross the road at those yellow road signs?

16. What was the best thing before sliced bread?

17. If you try to fail, and succeed, which have you done?

18. If one synchronized swimmer drowns, do the rest drown too?

Day 7

*This story necessitates acting as well as story telling. Without the body antics during the telling, this joke loses MOST of its flair. So, as the teller, you must become both the blind man and the manager. If you're telling this to a school age group, I advise starting by making sure they have seen people with seeing-eye dogs, refresh their memories as to how the dogs are used (i.e. what kind of information the dog provides the human), and perhaps tell the story as if it really happened to you. It's another one of my **true stories**.*

The Blind Shopper

A man, apparently blind, enters a clothing store. Beside him, he has a Labrador Retriever, which is on a harness. The dog leads the man to the approximate center of the store, stops, and sits down. The blind man then reaches into his pocket, pulls out a leash, takes the harness off the dog, and attaches the leash to the dog's collar.

This accomplished, the blind man heaves the dog up into his arms, and then in one fluid motion, throws the dog skyward and proceeds to whip the dog around his head which is now circling above the man's head 360 degrees, like a propeller. The dog begins howling. Each rotation, the dog howls something like "Owwwowww!"

People in the store are understandably scared, stunned, aghast, and some are even angry at what appears to be inhumane treatment of the dog that continues to howl.

An inexperienced clerk runs to get the manager of the store. The manager immediately returns and carefully approaches the blind man.

"Sir, sir!" says the manager. He is close enough to have to duck out of the way each time the dog passes overhead. "Um, this is a little unusual for our store!"

The blind man keeps twirling his dog, which keeps howling. "Owwwowww!"

"Um, sir, sir? I'm sorry but your behavior is most unsettling for our other customers," says the frantic manager. He still must keep ducking to avoid being hit.

The blind man says nothing. Meanwhile, the dog keeps howling, "Owwwowww!"

The manager pleads, "Sir, sir, is there something I can help you with?

Finally, the blind man says, "No thanks, just looking around."

Day 8

*Speaking of dogs, most people have had some experience with having a dog as a pet, or at least knowing someone who does. For us dog lovers, we **marry** them for better or worse. While I'm of the opinion most is "better," dogs certainly exhibit some behaviors that we would not tolerate from our kids, or even, our wife. So, perhaps it's time there be some…*

Rules for Dogs

1. The garbage collector is not stealing our stuff.

2. I do not need to suddenly stand straight up when I'm lying under the coffee table.

3. I will not roll my toys behind the fridge, behind the sofa or under the bed.

4. I will shake rainwater off my fur before entering the house.

5. I will not eat the cat's food before they eat it or after they throw it up.

6. I will not throw up in the car.

7. I will not roll on dead animals just because I like the way they smell.

8. "Kitty box crunchies" although tasty, are not considered food.

9. The diaper pail is not a cookie jar.

10. I will not bark when I hear the doorbell on television.

11. My head does not belong in the refrigerator.

12. I will not greet visitors to our house by sticking my nose near their privates.

13. I will not use family t.v. time as an occasion to pass gas.

14. The toilet bowl is not my water dish.

16. Suddenly turning around to smell my rear end is not polite.

17. An open car door is not my personal invitation to go on a ride.

18. The cat is not a squeaky toy. Squeezing him until he makes that noise is not good.

Day 9

Most kids don't know the difference between an atheist and an agnostic. A lot of adults don't either. The following story provides some humor in helping students remember the concept of atheism. In any event, before you tell the story, make sure your audience understands the definition of **atheism.**

The Atheist

An atheist was taking a walk in the woods in Alaska enjoying the marvels of evolution. But he kept getting the feeling he was being watched.

Alongside a river, he heard a rustling in the bushes and looked up in time to see an enormous grizzly bear watching him. He walked faster and faster, as did the grizzly until he was jogging and the bear was loping.

Finally, he broke into a sprint, spying a tree ahead he hoped he could jump into branches he could climb to safety. The bear was gaining on him. He almost reached the tree when his foot was snagged by a root, and down he went. He rolled to see the bear on him with a mighty paw raised to strike him. At that instant, the atheist cried, "Oh my God!"

Time stopped. The bear froze. The forest was silent. Even the river stopped flowing.

As a bright light shone upon the man, a voice came out of the sky: "You deny my existence for all of these years; teach others I don't exist, and even credit creation to a cosmic accident. Do you expect me to help you out of this predicament? Am I to count you as a believer now?"

The atheist looked directly into the light: "It would be hypocritical of me to suddenly ask You to treat me as a Christian now, but perhaps you could make the bear a Christian?"

"Very well," the voice said.

The bright light disappeared, the breeze resumed, and the river started to flow again.

Then, the bear dropped his right paw, brought it together with his left, bowed his head, and spoke, "Lord, you are a gracious God. Thank you for providing me with this nourishment that I am about to take. Amen!"

Day 10

For students, this joke works best if they have had some experiences with lab dissections (background/previous knowledge). However, you don't want to tip them off with that reference. What you may have to explain is the concept of "psychic" and how some people seek the abilities of fortune tellers, psychics, astrologists, etc. to find out what their future holds.

Frog on the Psychic Hotline

Recently, the Psychic Hotline and Psychic Friends Network have launched hotlines for frogs. Here is the story of one frog and his discussion with a psychic.

A frog telephones the Psychic Hotline and is told, "You are going to meet a beautiful young girl who will want to know everything about you."

The frog says, "This is fantastic! Will I meet her at a party? Is she going to kiss me and turn me into a prince?"

"No," says the psychic, "You will meet her next semester in her biology class."

Day 11

Ever enjoyed the embarrassment of not knowing what's going on, but being in the midst of people who do? And then, despite our ignorance, we get a bit judgmental about the behavior of those in the know? The following does a good job of illustrating this in a fun manner.

Football Confusion

A young man invites his girlfriend to a football game. She's excited as she's never been to a game and knows nothing about it. She's looking forward to her boyfriend explaining.

At the beginning of the game, the captains meet in the center of the field for the toss of the coin - a quarter. The winner of the toss is announced and the crowd starts going crazy. The kickoff ensues and the girl gets caught up in the excitement and cheers along with everyone else.

After the game, the boyfriend says, "Well, you seemed to get into the game - What did you think?"

The girl says, "Well, it was fun, but to be honest I thought it was a little silly."

"What do you mean?" the boyfriend questions.

"Well, come on," she says. "All that for a quarter? I mean, I felt stupid yelling, 'Get the quarter back' for the whole 3 hours."

Day 12

Corny! Despite everybody claiming a joke is too corny, the fact remains that corny jokes survive. And, if truth be told, people laugh at them despite their groans and protestations of "Oh, that is so corny!" Then, they secretly rush off and tell it to someone else. So, okay, this one is corny. Don't take yourself too seriously.

The Literate Frog

A pair of chickens walk into a public library, proceed to the checkout desk with a couple of books under their wings and say, "Buk, buk, buk, buk." The librarian asks to see their library card, which they produce, so she checks out the books.

The next day, the same scenario. "Buk, buk, buk," cluck the chickens, and she once again checks out the books.

On the third day, she gets a bit suspicious when the same two chickens come in and check out still more books. So she secretly follows them as they leave.

After quite some time, the chickens lead the librarian to a marsh. She watches the chickens from behind a tree. The chickens throw the books into the pond in the center of the marsh. Each time they do, a frog, which sits in the very center, looks at the title, and then says, "Rrrrredit, Rrrredit, Rrrredit!"

Day 13

This is a great story for emphasizing the importance of accurate communication. Did we say what we meant to communicate, or did we say something that can be taken more than one way? This joke illustrates the point.

A Hunter calls 9-1-1

Recently, two hunters were traipsing through thick cover in search of their prey. One of the two hunters was somewhat overweight, had not conditioned himself for the strenuous activity, and was suffering from the high elevation. Suddenly, he keeled over and appeared to be suffering from a heart attack.

His buddy hadn't taken any CPR training and panicked. However, he remembered his cell phone in his pack. Remarkably, being close to a summit, he had cell coverage, so he dialed 9-1-1.

An operator came on almost immediately, but it appeared that it was too late. His friend had turned ashen gray, was salivating, his eyes stared straight into the heavens, and there was no appearance of breathing. The operator said, "This is 9-1-1. Do you have an emergency?"

The panicked hunter said, "I'm out in the middle of nowhere, and my friend had a heart attack, I think. I don't know what to do! I think he's dead."

The operator said, "Sir, calm down. I'm here to help you. But before I give you any guidance, you need to make sure."

"Okay, just a minute," said the hunter. The 9-1-1 operator waited for a minute and then she heard what sounded like three shots. Then after another moment, the panicked voice came back on the line.

"Okay, he's dead for sure. Now what?"

Day 14

Often, humor is found in words that can have two meanings – even if the confusion is caused by pronunciation - a good object lesson in homonyms.

Cool Hand Fido

A dog wanders into a bar. He sidles up to the bar counter, and takes himself a stool.

The bartender walks over and glares at him. "What do you want?" the bartender asks, with a hard edge to his voice.

"Give me a glass of water – neat," says the dog.

"We don't serve dogs in this here bar," says the bartender in a menacing voice.

The dog leaves, with his tail between his legs. But still, he's kind of indignant.

The next day, the same dog enters the same bar, approaches the bar, takes a stool and stares evenly at the bartender.

The bartender is surprised at the dog's return, but angry, nonetheless. "What do *you* want?"

"I'll have a glass of water – over the rocks," says the dog.

The bartender is incensed at the dog's nerve. "I told you we don't serve your type in this here bar! Now get outa' here before I get violent!"

The dog stands, stares hard into the bartender's eyes, then slowly backs toward the door, and leaves.

The next day, the dog comes in, walks brazenly up to the bar, plunks himself down in a stool, and barks, "Bartender! Get me a water!"

The bartender, who had his back to the door, whirls around, and can't believe his eyes! He reaches under the counter by the cash register, pulls out a revolver, and in one fluid motion, cocks the gun, aims, and shoots the dog in the foot!

The dog howls in pain, and runs out of the bar yelping.

A week goes by. Then two weeks, and a third. About a month later, the dog struts into the bar, this time wearing two holsters, filled with a pair of silver Colt .45s that have pearl handles. He approaches the bar, walking like a Texan.

This time, the regular bartender is not there; instead it's his wife. She smiles at the dog and asks, "May I help you?"

The dog looks around, sizes up the situation, and then drawls,

"Yeah. I'm here to see the man who shot my Paw!"

Day 15

And how about a political joke? This one can be told several ways: Republican, Democrat, Independent, Conservative, Liberal. So, no matter which way I write, somebody is going to be ticked at me. Well, get over it.

What's the Difference?

One day during his presidency, Bill Clinton was jogging around the Mall, which stretches, between the Capitol and the Lincoln Memorial. (His secret service agents were with him, of course – both to protect the President as well as potential interns in the White House. Anyway, I digress.)

As he rounded one of the corners, a young boy had a box full of puppies he was trying to give away. The President took a breather and decided to encourage the boy for his work ethic and compassion (to the dogs).

"Hello there, son. How's business?" asked the President.

"Wow, you're the President!" said the boy. Clinton chuckled, enjoying the apparent admiration. "Mr. President," said the boy, "would you like to have a puppy? They're free!"

"Thank you very much for the kind offer," said President Clinton, "but I already have a dog - Buddy. One dog is all we need in the White House."

"But, Mr. President, you should have another dog. Besides, these dogs are *Democrat* dogs."

From this, the President got a big laugh, clearly appreciating the boy's quick thinking and marketing. However, he remained steadfast, and after again thanking the boy for the offer, continued his jog.

When he got home, he told First Lady, Hilary, all about it. She, too, thought this was *hilarious*, and they recounted the story to several friends.

About 3 weeks later, Hilary was out for a walk on the Mall and spied a boy with a box of young dogs. She felt this must be the same boy, so she approached him ready for similar treatment and a good, shared laugh.

"Hello! Are you the young man who offered my husband, the President, a puppy?" Hilary asked.

"Yes," the boy said flatly, looking down, avoiding eye contact. He obviously wasn't warming up to the First Lady.

Hilary was a little taken aback at the cool reception. "Well, they sure are cute," she said, almost inviting him to offer one to her.

"Yeah," the boy said kind of nonchalantly. "They are that." And he continued to remain aloof.

Hilary became a little more than a bit annoyed. "Well, aren't you going to offer one to me?" she asked, fighting to keep the agitation from showing in her voice. "I understand from my husband that these are *Democrat* puppies!"

"Well," the boy said, "you wouldn't want one of these dogs, maam. Trust me."

Now, Hilary was ticked at this impudent rejection. "And why is that?" she demanded. "They're Democrats!" she said somewhat desperate at the degrading situation.

"Well, that was a few weeks ago," the boy explained. "Since then, their eyes have opened."

Day 16

Supposedly, these are actual titles from newspaper articles. Don't ask for any citations proving authenticity – I have none. In any event, they're pretty funny. These can be read, projected, or used as occasional illustrative points of confusion. It's sort of like the Blue Laws I keep posted in my class. Students are encouraged to imagine the circumstances that might have led to legislators coming up with laws that seem so bizarre; the same is true of these titles – what events led to the title?

News Titles

Dealers to Hear Car Talk at Noon

Chef Throws Heart into Helping to Feed the Needy

Arson Suspect Held in Massachusetts Fire

Lansing Residents Drop off Trees

British Union Finds Dwarfs in Short Supply

Teacher Lends Hand to Needy Student

Actor Sent to Jail for not Finishing Sentence

Sun or Rain Expected During the Day, Dark Tonight

Study Shows that Teenage Pregnancy Drops Significantly after age 25

Specialist Says Electric Chair can be Extremely Painful

Teen Girls Often Have Babies Fathered by Men

Yankees Take Walk to Tie Store

Lack of Brains Hinders Research

Local Tourists Have Plenty Do Do Here

Miners Refuse to Work After Death

Man Steals Clock, Faces Time

Grandmother of Eight Makes Hole in One

Study Shows Milk Drinkers Turning to Powder

Typhoon Rips through Graveyard; Hundreds Dead

Child's Stool Great for Garden Use

Autos Kill 110 a Day; Let's Resolve to Do Better

Astronaut to Blame for Gas in Spacecraft

Drunk Man Gets Nine Months in Violin Case

Day 17

True or not? Again, I don't know. Just pose it as something that was passed along on the internet – then you're not trying to validate credibility. But maybe it did happen. If so, I wouldn't want to be the school that faced the investigation.

Lipstick in School

According to a news report, a certain school in Garden City, MI was recently faced with a unique problem.

A number of 12-year-old girls were beginning to use lipstick and would apply it in the washroom. That was fine, but after they put on their lipstick, they would press their lips to the mirror to blot it and would leave dozens of lip prints. Every night, the maintenance man would remove them and the next day, the girls would repeat the process.

Finally, the principal decided that something had to be done. He called all the girls to the washroom and met them there with the maintenance man. He explained that all these lip prints were causing a major problem for the custodian who had to clean the mirrors every night.

To demonstrate how difficult it had been to clean the mirrors, he asked the maintenance man to show the girls how much effort was required. The custodian obliged, took out a long-handled squeegee, dipped it in the toilet, and cleaned the mirror with it.

Since then, there have been no lip prints on the mirror.

Day 18

Okay, another political joke. This time, I'll try to balance out the situation (based on my previous fun with Democrats). This time I'll reverse the roles. Okay? Happy?

Brain Dead

A young lady found her uncle unconscious and lying on the floor of his house.

She immediately called for an ambulance, and he was put into intensive care.

After a while a grim faced doctor came out and said, "I'm sorry - your uncle's brain is dead, but his heart is still beating."

The poor lady blanched, put her hand to her cheek and exclaimed, "Oh my! We've never had a Republican in our family before!"

Day 19

Courage and its cost – this is a topic I frequently discuss in American History. Enjoy!

The Cost of Courage

A man appeared before St. Peter at the pearly gates. "Have you ever done anything of particular merit?" St. Peter asked.

"Well, yes," the man offered. "On a trip to the Black Hills out in South Dakota, I came upon a gang of high-testosterone bikers, who were threatening a young woman.

"I directed them to leave her alone, but they wouldn't listen. So, I approached the largest and most heavily tattooed biker and smacked him on the head, kicked his bike over, ripped out his nose ring, and threw it on the ground."

I yelled, "Now, back off! Or you'll answer to me!"

St. Peter was impressed: "When did this happen?"

"Just a couple minutes ago."

Day 20

*Is a wrong still a wrong depending on who is committing it? Of course!
Do we treat different people differently – do some get preferential
treatment? Duh. Okay, here's a good starter for a discussion on this
topic.*

Who's Your Limo Driver?

After getting all of Billy Graham's luggage loaded into the limo,
the driver noticed that Mr. Graham was still standing on the curb.

"Excuse me, Mr. Graham," said the driver, "would you please
take your seat so we can leave?"

"Well, to tell you the truth," said Mr. Graham, "they never let me
drive anymore, and I'd really like to drive today."

"I'm sorry but I cannot let you do that. I'd lose my job! And what
if something should happen?" protested the driver, wishing he'd never
gone to work that morning.

"There might be something extra in it for you," said Mr. Graham.

Reluctantly, the driver got in the back as Billy Graham climbed in
behind the wheel. The driver quickly regretted his decision when, after
exiting the airport, Mr. Graham floored it, accelerating the limo to 105
mph.

"Please slow down, sir!!!" pleaded the worried driver, but Billy
kept the pedal to the metal until they heard sirens.

"Oh, man, I'm gonna' lose my license," moaned the driver.

Billy pulled over and rolled down the window as the cop
approached, but the cop took one look at him, went back to his

motorcycle, and got on the radio.

"I need to talk to the Chief," he said to the dispatcher. The Chief got on the radio and the cop told him that he'd stopped a limo going a hundred and five.

"So bust him," said the Chief.

"I don't think we want to do that, he's really important," said the cop.

Then the Chief exclaimed, "All the more reason!"

"No, I mean really important," said the cop. The Chief then asked, "Who ya' got there, the Mayor?"

Cop: "Bigger."

Chief: "Governor?"

Cop: "Bigger."

"Well," said the Chief, "who is it?"

Cop: "I think it's God!"

Chief: "What makes you think it's God?"

Cop: " He's got Billy Graham for a limo driver!"

Day 21

This one is for math teachers! How many concepts do you teach wherein your learners just stare back at you with that deer-in- the-headlight look? One of my close friends is a math teacher, and there was one class he taught wherein his students asked absolutely no questions, would not participate when called upon, and showed zero reaction to any of his hilarious antics. So, Jeff, this one's for you!

12 Brazilian Soldiers Killed

A man was sitting on the train reading the newspaper. The headline blared,
"12 Brazilian Soldiers Killed."

He shook his head at the sad news, then turned to the stranger sitting next to him and asked, "How many is a Brazilian?"

Day 22

*At some point in the year, my American History students will begin asking questions about forms of government. It usually starts when they finally learn what **a republic** is – having recited it in the Pledge of Allegiance since kindergarten. Anyway, here's a simplistic, albeit funny, explanation.*

Cows and Politics

• SOCIALIST

You have two cows. The government takes one and gives it to your neighbor. You form a cooperative to tell him how to manage his cow.

• COMMUNIST

You have two cows. The government seizes both and provides you with milk. You wait in line for hours to get it. It is expensive and sour.

• DEMOCRACY - AMERICAN

You have two cows. The government taxes you to the point you have to sell both to support a man in a foreign country who has only one cow, which was a gift from your government.

• CAPITALISM, AMERICAN

You have two cows. You sell one, buy a bull, and build a herd of cows.

• DEMOCRAT

You have two cows. Your neighbor has none. You feel guilty for being successful. Barbara Streisand sings for you.

• REPUBLICAN

You have two cows. Your neighbor has none. So?

• AMERICAN CORPORATION

You have two cows. You sell one, lease it back to yourself and do an IPO on the 2nd one. You force the two cows to produce the milk of four cows. You are surprised when one cow drops dead. You spin an announcement to the analysts stating you have downsized and are reducing expenses. Your stock goes up.

• GERMAN CORPORATION

You have two cows. You engineer them so they are all blond, drink lots of beer, give excellent quality milk, and run a hundred miles an hour. Unfortunately they also demand 13 weeks of vacation per year.

• FRENCH CORPORATION

You have two cows. You go on strike because you want three cows. You go to lunch and drink wine. Life is good.

• JAPANESE CORPORATION

You have two cows. You redesign them so they are one-tenth the size of an ordinary cow and produce twenty times the milk. They learn to travel on unbelievably crowded trains. Most are at the top of their class at cow school.

Day 23

Spelling errors continues to plague the writing of our youth, not to mention adults who have already finished their formal education. To complicate matters, language continues to evolve. If you were hoping for permanent standardization, forget it! The following clearly illustrates my point.

Spelling Rules

The European Commission announced an agreement whereby English will be the official language of the European Union rather than German - the other possibility.

In negotiations, the British Government conceded that English spelling had room for improvement, accepting a 5-year phase-in plan resulting in "Euro-English".

In the first year, "s" will replace the soft "c." Sertainly, this will make the sivil servants jump with joy.

The hard "c" will be dropped in favour of "k." This should klear up konfusion, and keyboards kan have one less letter.

There will be growing publik enthusiasm in the sekond year when the troublesome "ph" will be replaced with "f." This will make words lik e fotograf 20% shorter.

In the 3rd year, publik akseptanse of the new spelling kan be expekted to reach the stage where more komplikated changes are possible.

Governments will enkourage the removal of double letters which have always ben a deterent to akurate speling.

Also, al wil agre that the horibl mes of the silent "e" in the languag is disgrasful and it should go away.

By the 4th yer people wil be reseptiv to steps such as replasing "th" with "z" and "w" with "v."

During ze fifz yer, ze unesesary "o" kan be dropd from vords kontaining "ou" and after ziz fifz yer, ve vil hav a reil sensi bl riten styl.

Zer vil be no mor trubl or difikultis and evrivun vil find it ezi tu understand ech oza. Ze drem of a united urop vil finali kum tru.

Und efter ze fifz yer, ve vil al be speking German like zey vunted in ze forst plas!

Day 24

Another true story – sort of. This one is a lot of fun to be theatrical, embellish, go through lots of gestures and theatrics. Always gets at least one cat lover.

Gas on a Cat

A terrific windstorm swept the Northwest, knocking down trees with just no regard to the work it might cause me. Unfortunately, I didn't have a chainsaw, so I went to my neighbor's house in hopes of borrowing his.

My neighbor was very accommodating. Let me borrow it, reminded me how to use it, even loaned my the 2 cycle oil for the gas.

His cat followed me home. Now, cats seem to know who doesn't like them all that much and get a great deal of satisfaction out of lavishing attention on that person. Anyway, the cat was rubbing up against my legs and purring while I was standing in the backyard getting the chainsaw ready for duty.

While I was trying to fill up the tiny little gas opening with gas, I accidentally spilled. Down flowed the combustive liquid onto said cat.

Suffice it to say that gas burns the skin. But what happened next was beyond belief. The cat let out a yowl such as I've never heard before. It continued to do so while hissing something fierce.

My wife came to the back door, opened the slider to see what was the matter. The cat took that as an invitation inside, streaked past my wife who stood wide-eyed at the oncoming feline freight train.

The cat no sooner entered the house, than my two dogs entered the chase. The cat appeared to be demoned possessed – meowing, hissing, spitting, and climbing everything in sight – both in attempt to escape from the dogs and what we could only surmise was intense pain from the gasoline on its skin.

Up the curtains it climbed – shredding them in the process. Over the banister, up the beams supporting the ceiling, down the hall – somehow cutting the corners so tightly that it took up to the sides of the walls like banked turns on a race track.

All the while, the dogs were in hot pursuit, barking and baying in anticipation of catching this demented cat.

Finding no escape route at the end of the hall, the cat made an abrupt u-turn and headed back into our direction. Both my wife and I dove for cover.

The cat lighted upon the dining table, and then jumped to the chandelier hanging above the table. With all four paws, it latched onto the lighting fixture and hung, suspended, upside down. It was at this point, the cat, for the first time, ceased its frantic race.

While it was only for seconds, it seemed like slow motion compared to the earlier frenetic behavior. Then, the cat moaned, released its grip on the fixture, and fell, "smack," onto the table, rigid, with its paws outstretched to the ceiling. The poor kitty's eyes were rolled back into its head.

Apparently, it had run out of gas!

(No matter how many times I tell that joke, I have never had an audience fail me. If told with the proper dramatic flare, before you get to the last line, you pause and stare at the audience as if that's the end of the story. ALWAYS, someone will ask, "Was it dead?" That's your cue to give the last line. "No, apparently, it had just run out of gas.")

Day 25

Usually, as a teacher, I think my directions are so clear and easy to follow. "If people would just listen," I sometimes lament. The following falls into the category of "what the speaker meant to communicate" and "what the listener heard." Both are correct.

Marriage Counseling

A husband and wife go to a counselor after 15 years of marriage.

The counselor asks them what the problem is, and the wife goes into a tirade, listing every problem they have ever had in the 15 years they've been married. She goes on and on and on.

Finally, the counselor gets up, goes around the desk, embraces the woman and kisses her passionately. The woman shuts up and sits quietly in a daze.

The counselor turns to the husband and says, "That is what your wife needs at least three times a week. Can you do that?"

The husband thinks for a moment and replies, "Well, I can get her here Monday and Wednesday, but Friday I golf.

*This one has made the rounds for years. It's still as funny as ever. I have absolutely no idea as to its authenticity, but it could be adapted to **another true story**. The object lesson? Gravity works.*

Bricklayer's Accident Report

Dear Sir:

I am writing in response to your request for additional information in Block 3 of the accident report form. I put "poor planning" as the cause of my accident. You asked for a fuller explanation and I trust the following details will be sufficient.

I am a bricklayer by trade. On the day of the accident, I was working alone on the roof of a new six-story building. When I completed my work, I found that I had some bricks left over which, when weighed later were found to be slightly in excess of 500 lbs.

Rather than carry the bricks down by hand, I decided to lower them in a barrel by using a pulley, which was attached to the side of the building on the sixth floor.

Securing the rope at ground level, I went up to the roof, swung the barrel out and loaded the bricks into it. Then I went down and untied the rope, holding it tightly to ensure a slow descent of the bricks. You will note in Block 11 of the accident report form that I weigh

175lbs. Due to my surprise at being jerked off the ground so suddenly, I lost my presence of mind and forgot to let go of the rope. Needless to say, I proceeded at a rapid rate up the side of the building. In the vicinity of the third floor, I met the barrel which was now proceeding downward at an equally, impressive speed. This explained the fractured skull, minor abrasions and the broken collar bone, as listed in section 3 of the accident report form.

Slowed only slightly, I continued my rapid ascent, not stopping until the fingers of my right hand were two knuckles deep into the pulley. Fortunately by this time I had regained my presence of mind and was able to hold tightly to the rope, in spite of beginning to experience a great deal of pain.

At approximately the same time, however, the barrel of bricks hit the ground and the bottom fell out of the barrel. Now devoid of the weight of the bricks, that barrel weighed approximately 50 lbs. I refer you again to my weight. As you can imagine, I began a rapid descent, down the side of the building.

In the vicinity of the third floor, I met the barrel coming up. This accounts for the two fractured ankles, broken tooth and several lacerations of my legs and lower body.

Here my luck began to change slightly. The encounter with the barrel seemed to slow me enough to lessen my injuries when I fell into the pile of bricks and fortunately only three vertebrae were cracked.

I am sorry to report, however, as I lay there on the pile of bricks, in pain, unable to move, I again lost my composure and presence of mind and let go of the rope and I lay there watching the empty barrel begin its journey back down onto me. This explains the two broken legs.

I hope this answers your inquiry."

Day 27

Okay, we've all heard the "might be a redneck if" statements. Well for those readers who are school employees, these may speak to you.

YOU MAY BE A SCHOOL EMPLOYEE IF...

1. You believe the playground should be equipped with a Ritalin salt lick.

2. You want to slap the next person who says, "Must be nice to work 8 to 3:00 and have summers free."

3. You can tell if it's a full moon without looking outside.

4. You believe "shallow gene pool" should have its own check box on a report card.

5. When out in public you feel the urge to snap your fingers at children you do not know and correct their behavior.

6. You have no social life between August and June.

7. You believe that unspeakable evils will befall you if anyone says: "Boy, the kids sure are mellow today."

8. Marking all A's on report cards would make your life SO easy.

9. You think people should be required to get a government permit before being allowed to reproduce.

10. You can't have children because there's no name you could give a child that wouldn't bring on high blood pressure the moment you heard it.

11. You think caffeine should be available in intravenous form.

12. You wish you had taken more classes in diplomacy when a parent says, "I have a great idea I'd like to discuss. I think it would be such fun."

13. Meeting a child's parent instantly answers the question, "Why is this kid like this?"

Can you remember, absent-mindedly, doing anything dumb? If not, I think you have a memory problem or prefer lying over the truth. At the middle school level, kids live in dread fear of making a stupid move in front of their peer group. Accordingly, they can relate to this poor smuck.

That's Gotta' Hurt!

A man walked into his office to go to work. Both of his ears had enormous bandages on them. His boss did a double-take and went over to the man.

"Are you okay?" asked the boss.

"What?" said his employee.

The boss gestured to your ears. "What on earth happened?"

"Bad weekend," said the man with the bandaged ears. "I was ironing clothes. Boy, have you ever had one of those miserable experiences of losing your focus, making a split second mistake, and paying dearly for it?"

"Yeah," said the boss. "So what happened?"

"Well, like I said, I was ironing. I was smoothing out the pleats of my pants with my hands, the phone rang, I accidentally picked up the iron and placed it to my ear!"

"Oh my gosh!" said the boss. "That must have hurt like nobody's business."

"You're telling me!" said the man with the burned ears.

"But what happened to your other ear?" asked the boss.

"I was panicked, so I tried to call the doctor."

Day 29

Here's a good one to lighten up the mood prior to taking a test. Lots of students struggle with testing anxiety, and sometimes a little levity will reduce the tension.

How to Take a Test

A teacher had decided to make the final for his class a *true-false* test.

Towards the end of the class period, he looked up to see a student repeatedly tossing a coin up into the air. It was beginning to distract the students sitting to each side of him, so the teacher quietly walked back to the coin throwing student.

Leaning over and speaking quietly to avoid interrupting the other test takers, he said, "Son, may I ask what you are doing?"

The student maintained his concentration, flipping a single coin into the air, slapping it down on his wrist, and looking at it and his paper each time.

Then he looked up at the teacher and said, "I'm checking my answers."

Day 30

My class is pretty accustomed to me starting such a yarn with, "Hey, did I ever tell you the true story about the time…? After only a few of these, they will know that true story is code for "Okay, here comes another one of Brigleb's jokes." But in any event, they like the format; half of their brain is saying "Danger – he's about to tell a big fat lie" while the other half is struggling with wanting to get sucked in with "Really?"

*It's time for another dog story. This is a **true story**. (Yeah, right.)*

Whatta' Dog

I went to the movies this weekend. Everything would have been quite normal, except that unlike any previous visit to a cinema experience, this time there was a patron there who had brought his dog. I was thinking, "Oh what is this world coming to? Pets in the workplace, pet friendly stores – now in the movies, too?"

Well the movie was pretty good. But to tell you the truth, most of my attention wasn't on it. I was totally engrossed in the behavior of the dog. During the scary parts, the hair on the back of his neck stood up. When there were humorous parts, the dog seemed to smile, he stood up and wagged his tail. During a really sad part, his ears were down, he looked sadly at his owner and licked his face. At the end of the movie, the dog sat up on his haunches, lifted his front paws and seemed to bark his appreciation.

In the lobby, I hurriedly approached the dog and its owner. "Excuse me," I said. "but I just had to ask you about your dog."

"Yes?" the man said.

"Well, I couldn't believe me eyes! Your dog is incredible! I mean – he acted protective when the bad guy was being scary, he seemed really happy during the funny parts, sad at the sad parts, and really seemed to enjoy the whole movie!"

"I know, it surprised me too," said the dog owner. "He hated the book!"

Day 31

Observation is so important. I remember when I taught science, trying to impress this fact on my students. "Don't only notice the obvious," I would say. "Observe beyond what's calling your attention." As an object lesson, nobody is better than Sherlock Holmes.

A Night of Camping with Holmes and Watson

Sherlock Holmes and Doctor Watson decided to do something decidedly different from their routine of solving crimes. Uncharacteristically, they went camping.

Somewhere in the wee hours of the night, Holmes woke Watson.

"What? What is it, Holmes?" Watson implored.

"Take stock of our circumstances and tell me what you observe," Holmes instructed, remaining in bed and staring into the heavens.

"Oh, Holmes, isn't this a bit early for one of your famous object lessons?" Watson complained.

"It's important, Watson. Humor me," Holmes said.

"Well, I can see from the position of the Big Dipper that it must be past 2:00 A.M.," Watson noted.

"Anything else?" Holmes asked.

"From the slight bending of the tree tops, I would surmise there is a 10 kilometer per hour breeze coming from the southwest," added Watson.

"Anything else?" Holmes pressed.

Watson was getting a little frustrated. "The dew on my sleeping bag would indicate that the barometric pressure might be dropping."

Holmes sighed, and there was disappointed silence for a moment.

"For the love of country, Holmes! What on earth am I missing?" Watson pleaded.

"Watson, you idiot. Our tent has been stolen."

Day 32

Loyalty. Friendship. Survival. This story has crucial elements that make you wonder about your friends. When the going gets tough, who gets going?

How Fast is a Bear?

Two hikers were deep in the woods of the Canadian province of Alberta. As they were trekking along, one of the two got the eerie sensation they weren't alone.

"Did you hear that?" said the first hiker to the second.

"You mean that sound of a branch snapping?" asked the second.

They both slowly turned, and not more than 50 yards to their rear was an enormous grizzly bear, which was standing on its hind legs and staring straight at them, nostrils flaring.

The first hiker immediately sat down, removed his hiking boots, pulled out some jogging shoes and quickly began lacing them onto his feet.

The second hiker looked at his friend, dumbfounded. "What are you doing?" he asked. "You can't possibly outrun a grizzly!"

The first hiker didn't bother to look up. He just kept hurriedly tying his shoes. "You're right, I can't outrun him. But I'm pretty sure I can outrun you."

Day 33

What do you do in church when bored or uncomfortable with your surroundings or fellow church attendees? Why, read the bulletin, of course. The announcements provide an overview of activities. Supposedly, the following announcements were from actual church bulletins. These provide a case study for the importance of proofreading, editing, and command of basic grammar conventions.

Church Bulletin Announcements

• Don't let worry kill you! Allow the church to help.

• Thursday night: Potluck supper. Prayer and medication to follow.

• Remember in prayer the many who are sick of our church and community.

• For those of you who have children and don't know it, we have a nursery downstairs.

• The rosebud on the altar this morning is to announce the birth of David Jones, the sin of Rev. and Mrs. John Jones.

• This afternoon there will be a meeting in the south and north ends of the church. Children will be baptized at both ends.

• Tuesday at 4:00 P.M. there will be an ice cream social. All ladies giving milk, please come early.

• Easter Sunday: The Lewis family will lay an egg at the altar.

• Bean supper will be held on Tuesday evening in the church hall. Music will follow.

• Evening service: "What is Hell?" Come early and listen to choir practice.

Day 34

More heavy thoughts and things to ponder. A person could spend a whole day contemplating questions such as these.

Have you ever wondered...

Why is abbreviate such a long word?

What does one plant to grow a seedless watermelon?

Why are *apartments* so close together?

Why isn't phonetic spelled the way it sounds?

Why is only one company allowed to make the game *Monopoly*?

What would chairs look like if one's knees bent the other way?

Why do advertisers say *new and improved*? How can it be new if it's improved?

If someone invented instant water, what would one add?

Why do people look up when they think?

Why does one turn down the radio volume when driving and looking for an address?

If you were driving a vehicle at the speed of light, would headlights have any effect?

Why are wrong numbers never busy?

If pro is the opposite of con, is progress the opposite of Congress?

Why do they sterilize needles for lethal injections?

If a Smurf is choked, what color does he turn?

Day 35

Adolescents love gross stuff. I remember teaching in Orangevale, California. The heat of spring was upon us, and we enjoyed our fully un-air conditioned building, complete with…what on earth is that smell? Science Fair was over, and one of my charges had hidden his display behind the curtain where it captured the full heat of the southern exposure. And there, it fermented and rotted. The matter? Potatoes that had liquefied and then became rancid. Of note, once the offensive spud juice was pinpointed, every 13 year old in the room simultaneously said, "Oh GROSS!" and then they ran to it to get a better whiff. And that IS the truth!

A Nutritious Snack!

A guy and his friend go to visit his grandmother. While he's talking with his grandmother, his friend starts eating the peanuts on the coffee table. As the conversation seemed to go on and on, the friend eventually finished all of the peanuts.

As they were leaving, the friend said to the grandmother, "Thanks for the peanuts. They sure hit the spot."

"Oh, you're quite welcome, young man," said the grandma. "I'm just so glad someone could enjoy them. Ever since I've had dentures, the best I can do is to suck the chocolate off."

Day 36

*Ever walk into your classroom or place of business, knowing it's going to be **one of those days**? Well, sometimes, the best antidote is to face it, and find something to laugh at. So, if you sense this is going to be one of those days, perhaps you need to read these to your class, colleagues, co-workers, family, employees, dogs, - and then put them on notice.*

It's probably going to be a bad day if...

• You call the Suicide Prevention hotline and they put you on hold.

• You arrive at work and the 60 Minutes camera crew is there.

• You turn on the news to see emergency routes out of the city being displayed.

• Your twin forgets your birthday.

•You wake up thinking your waterbed leaked and remember you don't own one.

• Your car horn gets stuck while following the Hells Angels.

• The bird singing outside your bedroom window is a buzzard.

Day 37

Stress! It's just so stressful. What to do with it? Well, here are some suggestions that you won't hear from a psychologist. (But only because they work, and the shrink would lose patients if he told you.)

Coping with Stress

Hold a fork right in front of your eyes while staring a people in the distance; pretend they're in jail.

See how much of a car you can polish with your earwax.

Try driving to work in reverse.

Pay a bill in pennies.

Tape a picture of someone you don't like on a watermelon and drop it off a high building. Try saying, "Bombs away!"

Fill out your tax forms in Roman Numerals.

Jam miniature marshmallows into your nose and sneeze them out. See how many, and how far.

Day 38

One of the classes I've taught over the years in middle school is designed for students who learn English as their second language. It presents a lot of opportunities to laugh at the misunderstandings which invariably occur while trying to communicate. You know, like, idiomatic expressions. Or simply, elevating one's volume to help the hearer better understand concepts. Just doesn't work. Anyway, one tactic that seems to be universal is observing what others do and then copying their behavior. It's gotta' work, doesn't it?

Just Do What *Everyone* Else Does

A missionary from the US went to Central America. He struggled with the language of the native speakers, and didn't seem to understand much of what was being said around him. Upon visiting one of the local churches, he arrived late and found that the church was pretty much full. Finally, somebody kindly helped him find a seat in the front row.

He didn't want to appear foolish, so he decided to copy the actions of the man sitting next to him. As the congregation sang and clapped, the missionary tried to sing along and clapped in unison with the others. When the man stood up to pray, the missionary followed suit. When the man took the cup and bread for the Lord's Supper, the missionary copied his every move. During the preaching, the missionary understood almost nothing, but he nodded and made facial expressions mimicking the man next to him.

Toward the end of the service, it seemed that the preacher was making announcements. People would occasionally clap, so the missionary clapped as well. At one point, the preacher said some more things, and the man next to the missionary stood up, so the missionary stood as well. The congregation became deathly silent, a few people even gasped. The missionary looked around and saw that no one else was standing, so he sat down.

As people were filing out of the church, the preacher stood at the door shaking hands with each person. When the missionary greeted him, the preacher said in English, "I take it you do not speak Spanish."

The missionary said, "No, I don't. How did you know?"

"Well," said the pastor, "I knew it when I announced that the Gonzalez family had had a new baby and invited the proud father to stand up."

Day 39

Do you like reading good stories? Of course you do – otherwise you wouldn't be reading this. Do you like judging a book by its cover? How do you feel about catchy titles? Here are some you may not want your children to read:

8 Childhood Titles to Avoid

Clifford the Big Dog is Put to Sleep

Protein in Your Nose

Charley Manson and His Bedtime Stories

How to Intimidate Your Classmates on the Playground

Curious George Finds a High-Voltage Fence

Things Rich Kids Have, But You Never Will

The Care Bears Maul Some Campers

Piano Keys – Is that You, Babar?

Day 40

Do you like puns? I sure do. You know – how electricity is a shocking subject; how you can really get plugged into it; how it can be both positive and negative but rarely neutral; how it's a current subject; how it's good to be grounded in the subject; how people get a charge from your jokes – you know, puns? Anyway, here you go…

Very Punny!

My first job was working in an orange juice factory, but I got canned. I just couldn't concentrate.

Then, I went to work in the woods as a lumberjack, but I couldn't hack it, so they gave me the axe.

After that, I tried to become a tailor, but I wasn't suited for it. Oh well, it was a sew-sew job anyway.

I then tried working at a muffler factory. It was exhausting.

So, I tried being a chef. I figured it would add some spice to my life, but I just couldn't find the thyme.

Maybe being a deli worker would be easier, I thought. Anyway I sliced it, I just couldn't cut the mustard.

Next, I tried to become a musician. It had a nice tempo, but I wasn't noteworthy.

A doctor? Nah, I didn't think I'd have the patience.

I love to fish, and I thought about becoming a professional fisherman. That almost hooked me. But I decided I wouldn't be able to live on the net income.

At that point, I decided to get employment in the local gym, but they said I wasn't fit for the job.

Starbucks gave me a shot working there, but then I just couldn't stand the grind.

Finally, I ended up as a historian. My friends tell me there's no future in it.

Day 41

*Ever notice how there are unwritten **rules** governing one's behavior on an elevator? Think about it – there are rules: Face the doors, don't make conversation with strangers, stare at the floor or the buttons on the wall or the numbers above the doors being illuminated. And if you sneeze, excuse yourself to no one in particular. But what if your goal was to purposely annoy people?*

Fun on an Elevator

• Make racecar noises when anyone gets on or off.

• Blow your nose and offer to show the contents to other passengers.

• Whistle the first seven notes to "It's a Small World" incessantly.

• Crack open your briefcase, stare inside and ask, "Do you have enough air?"

• Offer nametags to the other passengers.

• Stand facing one of the back corners, silent and motionless.

• At your floor, grunt and strain to open the doors, act embarrassed when they open.

• Greet people warmly with a handshake and ask them to address you as *Admiral*.

• Do Tai Chi exercises.

• Grin at other passengers for 30 seconds, then announce, "I have new socks on!"

• Show someone that you can put a quarter in your nose.

• Hold your legs together tightly and squirm uncomfortably. Then say, "Oops."

- Ask other passengers if your wound looks infected.

- Get in the elevator and set a box between the doors.

- Stare at a passenger for a while, then ask, "Are you one of them?"

- Wear a hand puppet and talk to the passengers with it.

- Say "Ding!" at each floor.

- Draw a square on the floor using chalk and then announce, "This is my personal space."

- Make explosion noises when another passenger pushes a button.

Day 42

Have you ever wondered what Heaven will be like, and even had conversations with someone about it. You know, like, "Gee, I really hope there is flyfishing in Heaven..."

Baseball in Heaven?

Two elderly gentlemen, Abe and Ben, were sitting on a park bench together. They both loved baseball like there was no tomorrow. Both had played in their youth, and since their friendship had begun years ago, they had gone to baseball games together on a regular basis.

As they sat there, Ben broke the silence. "Do you think there will be baseball in Heaven, Abe?"

"I've thought about that, Ben," said Abe. "I sure hope so."

"Listen, Abe," said Ben, "one of us is gonna' go first. Know what I mean?"

"Yeah," said Abe sadly. "I've thought about that too."

"Well, Abe, how about we strike a deal? Whichever of the two of us goes first, we promise that we'll do whatever we can to get back to visit the other and let him know if there's gonna' be baseball in Heaven. That way, the guy still living can start looking forward to Heaven and all." Ben finished his plan.

Abe smiled. "Deal," he said. "And that's a great idea."

Well, the very next week, old Abe was struck with a heart attack and died almost instantly. Ben was very sad, but knew that if Abe could, he'd be sure to visit with the promised piece of news.

Within another week, Ben was snoring soundly one night when he felt some sort of spiritual nudge. And then there was a spiritual voice. "Ben, Ben," said the voice. "It's your old friend Abe. I got news."

Instantly, Ben sat bolt upright in bed. He couldn't see his friend, but he could feel his presence. "Abe, Is it really you? Did you bring me good news?"

"Yes, Ben. It's really me. And I've brought you good news, and not-so-good news."

"Oh my," said Ben. "I can't wait any longer. Is there baseball in Heaven, Abe?"

"Yes, Ben. We have baseball in Heaven."

"Oh, what a relief. After that piece of news, what could possibly be bad?"

"Well, Ben," Abe said, "you're pitching on Saturday."

Day 43

In school, sometimes the best laughs come, not from jokes, but from tests. Occasionally, answers will cause a teacher to smile, chuckle, and sometimes snort milk out one's nose. What follows is a sampling of some I've received via email.

Science Test Answers

• H_2O is hot water, CO_2 is cold.

• When you smell an odorless gas, it's probably carbon monoxide.

• Water is composed of two gins – oxygin and hydrogin. Oxygin is pure gin, hydrogin is gin and water.

• There are three kinds of blood vessels: arteries, vanes, and caterpillars.

• Blood flows down one leg and up the other.

• The moon is a planet just like earth – only deader.

• A super saturated solution is one that holds more than it can hold.

• The pistol of a flower is its only protection against insects.

• A fossil is an extinct animal. The older it is, the more extinct it is.

• The tides are a fight between the Earth and moon. All water tends towards the moon, because there is no water on the moon, and nature abhors a vacuum. I forget where the sun gets involved.

Day 44

When you're a kid, you can't wait to get older. When you're in your 20s, you pretty much think you're perfect. When you're in your 30s, you try to act wise and look down upon the people in their 20s who think they're perfect. After your 30s, you mostly worry about getting old, and constantly check out people in the next decade beyond you, to see what's next. If I live long enough, I wonder which of these guys I'll become.

Golfing Buddies

An elderly gentleman visited his doctor, complaining about his rapid loss of sight.

"I'm terribly sorry," the doctor told him. "Your vision is, indeed, deteriorating rapidly, and there is nothing I can do."

"I understand," the old man said, and then he began to silently cry.

"It must be awful," admitted the doctor.

"The worst part," said the patient, "is not being able to play golf again. I live for that game!"

"Have you played long?" asked the doctor.

"My whole life," said the patient.

Two weeks later, the doctor called the patient who was becoming blind. "Listen, I was wondering, how good of a golfer are you?"

The patient was surprised by the question but answered honestly, "Well, I was very good. At one time I almost went professional."

"So could you hit the ball blindfolded?" asked the doctor.

"Yeah, but what's your point?" asked the old man.

"Well, it's just an idea, but here it is. I have another patient who is struggling with Alzheimer's disease. He's a golfer, too, but not nearly as good. He needs some companionship and exercise. Do you think you'd enjoy getting out to golf with him acting as your eyes and guide you around the course?"

The old guy was delighted. "Boy, that would be just grand," he said. "Can you set it up?"

So the doctor did. The old man's wife drove him out to the course at the appointed time, found the other gentleman, and the two were set to play.

It was a bit awkward on the first tee, but all worked out fine as the sighted man lined the blind man up so he was aiming down the fairway. But neither man let this deter their interest.

The blind man took a few practice swings and then asked his new friend if he was ready to watch the shot. He was.

The blind man, through years of practice was able to swing mechanically, and contacted the ball perfectly with a delightful and resounding smack.

He then turned in the direction of his friend. "Did you see it?" the blind man asked.

"Sure did. What a beautiful, beautiful shot," said the man with Alzheimer's.

"Well, where did it go?" asked the blind man.

The man with Alzheimer's stared blankly in the direction of the first hole. "I forgot."

Day 45

*I like to tell the following story in the first person narrative, as if I once had a job as a reporter. It's another **true story**...*

Three Legged Pig

Did I ever tell you guys the *true story* of when I worked as a reporter for the local newspaper? No? I wasn't really very good at it. And my editor called me in and said, "Listen, Brigleb. The last few months have been really unproductive for you. You're either not finding good stories or doing a horrendous job of writing about what you find. So, while I hate to say this, you need to come up with something good NOW, or we're going to have to let you go."

I was devastated. Do you know how much pressure it is to come up with a great story when your boss is demanding it RIGHT NOW? Anyway, I sat at my desk for awhile, then decided to take a drive to think and hopefully come up with some material.

After a couple hours, I pulled over at a roadside gas station, absent-mindedly filling the tank while just staring off into space – dreading the inevitable firing I was facing. Then something caught my eye.

Across the highway, in a big farm field, I could see an animal grazing. The critter was strange. It had the profile of a pig, but something was not quite right. I jogged across the highway for a closer look. Sure enough, it was a pig, but... it had only three legs. Maybe, I thought, this could be the story my editor would like. There had to be a story here!

I hopped the fence, so that I might check a bit closer, and then looked around. Off in the distance, I saw a tractor moving up and down a field. I jogged toward the tractor, hoping the guy driving it was the owner of the pig. Catching up to it, I heralded the operator. He stopped.

"Listen, Mister. I'm sorry to interrupt your work, but I was wondering if I could ask you a question or two."

The farmer had one of those classical hick drawls one associates with country bumpkins. "Why sure, sonny. Fire away."

"Hey - that pig over there," I said pointing, "is that your pig?"

"Yep, Shore is. He's one fine peeg." (That was how he pronounced "pig.")

"Well, I didn't want to keep you from your work too long, but I was wondering if you could tell me about his leg," I enquired.

"Whatcha mean, his leg?" the farmer returned.

"Well, I couldn't help but notice that he's missing one, he's only got three."

"Oh dat. Yeah. Well, I tell you what, he's one fine peeg."

"Yeah, I'll bet," I said patiently. "But could you tell me what happened to his leg?"

The farmer got off his tractor. "Okay. Well, one time, I wuz out on my harvester, harvesting as it wuz. Da peeg, he's kinda' like a dog to me, well, he wuz tagging along behind. I got up on this sidehill lie with the rig, and, well, gravity done took its course. The tractor toppled catter wampus like, and in the process, I wuz pinned under its weight like some ole squashed bug. Anyways, my peeg, he comes over, digs under the tractor, uses his snout to grab my coat, see? Den, he pulls, and he pulls, and he pulls, and he pulls, and he pulls. I don't know how many pulls as I passed out and lost count. But, da ting is, and dis be the truth, my peeg pulled me out from a certain death of suffocation!" And with that, the farmer stared at me with eyes that seemed to ask, "Can you believe dat?"

So, I said, "Wow. That's amazing! So, what happened, exactly? Did the tractor shift and crush his leg?"

The farmer got an irritated look on his face and said, "NO! Dat ain't it!" And he shook his head as if to suggest I was really stupid.

"Well," I said, not wanting to annoy him, "could you tell me about what happened to the pig's leg?'

"Oh, dat," said the farmer. "Well, here 'tis. Why, one time, me and my family, we wuz all asleep, tighter than bugs in a rug. In the middle of the night, a candle fell over, and the house caught afire. Let me tell you, went up like a torch. Ceptin' we didn't know it seeing as how we wuz sleeping and such. Well, our faithful peeg, came up the stairs, just like on the old show "Lassie" and went from one room to the next. And I'm not making this up! Da peeg, he started with the chilluns and pulled each one down the stairs to safety. Then, of course, he came for me, and finally, my wife. Why, if it hadn't been for da peeg, we would have been just so many smokey sausages. But dat peeg saved our lives!" And with that, the farmer stared at me, wide-eyed, to see if I could hardly believe it.

"So, did the pig's leg get burned?" I asked. "Did he sacrifice his leg to save your family?"

The farmer looked at me like I was a dim-witted, incompetent moron, who couldn't understand the obvious. "NO! Dat ain't it!" he snapped.

At this point, I was pretty sure this might go on all day. I was THIS close to having a great story, and yet the farmer wasn't giving me the key part of the story. "Listen, Mister. I don't mean to be rude. But I'd really like to know what happened to the pig's missing leg. Could you please tell me?" I pleaded.

"Oh dat, sure," he said. Then he looked me square in the eye and confided his important truth. "Listen, friend. It's not a peeg like dat, dat comes around every day. Dat peeg is a faithful, loyal member of our family. Dat peeg is really something special…"

"So what happened?" I interrupted, thinking he was going off on another tangent.

"Well, when you get a peeg dat good, you don't think ya' just eat him all at once, do ya?"

As Porky Pig used to say,

"That's All, Folks!"

At least for now. But hey, that was only a quarter's worth. And everybody knows that a school year lasts a lot longer than a quarter, or 45 days. In fact, if my math is right, a quarter is only,

something like, half of the year.

So, watch for coming attractions. Future release:

A (Second) Quarter's Worth of Humor.

But for now, so long! May the wind be at your back, the sunshine in your face, and your hair free of insects.

About the Author

James Brigleb is the husband of Linda, and father of Elisabeth, Alison, Rebekah, Jack, and grandfather to Joanna and Jacqueline. For the past 28 years, he has spent the majority of his days in classrooms, having the privilege of teaching adolescents. Brigleb currently lives in Wenatchee, Washington and enjoys pastimes of writing, motorcycling, and flyfishing.

For more James Brigleb fun, visit: joebananasez.com

www.ingramcontent.com/pod-product-compliance
Lightning Source LLC
Chambersburg PA
CBHW031523040426
42445CB00009B/363